Thank you for your
love and support
philip (since 1st grade)

Ritu Kaur   10/21/2017

Waves

ISBN-13: 978-0692958490
ISBN-10: 0692958495

I thank the universe for helping me find inspiration
Within myself
I thank Mummy Ji for giving me strength
I thank Anshi for her empathy and endless hours
Of reading and editing my work when no one else
Believed in me
I thank Mannu for his resilience to be himself
I thank Dev and my stepfather
For being strong men when I've needed them
And I thank all of you supporters
For taking the time to read my story

— *Grateful And Abundant*

Waves

Ritu Kaur

A Collection of Poetry & Prose

What's the first thing you notice about someone?
Me: *How well they listen.*

— *Two Ears, One Mouth*

I am not afraid
Of the dark
I find it comforting
The darkness and I
Understand one another
Through every unlit corner
In every dark room
Through each black place
That exists
Darkness is present
Before light will ever be
Black holes are meant to
Consume you
But I think I would feel
More alive
Traveling through a black hole
Perhaps there, I'd find my soul
People say
You should not fear the dark
You should only fear what is
Inside of it
I beg to differ
I only fear
What is outside of it

Day 1: Mummy Ji got blamed. The social workers
thought we'd be unsafe with her. They took us to a
daycare center offering us gifts and dinner. Then had us
individually examined by the nurse. I was 11 years old.
Mannu was 9. Dev, 6. Anshi, 5. We had a long drive to
Vallejo, where we were placed in a home with Black
parents for the next ten days. I had a separate room from
Mannu, Dev, and Anshi. But it gave me comfort
knowing my siblings were sleeping together. If they
could sleep. Foster parents and I had an argument that
night, while questions lingered in my mind. Then off to
bed to silently cry.
Day 2 was blurry and unreal. One of the foster boys
followed me around and tried to kiss me. He shared a
room with my siblings which baffled me. Foster parents
wouldn't allow me to switch rooms with him. It was
lonelier than ever.
Day 3: Empty stomachs went to bed each night 'cause
most people forget that vegetarians don't only eat stir
fry. The social worker let us talk to Mummy Ji over the
phone. Foster parents timed our four minute
conversation and restricted us from speaking to her in
our mother tongue.
Night 4: Dev had to share a bed with the boy who tried
to kiss me. Dev was afraid of him so he slept next to me.
Day 5: We got in trouble for it. I had cramps later on that
night. I felt a drip in my underwear. That was the day I
discovered. I was a woman.
Day 6: Dev had long, beautiful hair that I still didn't
know how to take care of. I tried to do his hair like
Mummy Ji had for years but failed. We went to a Black
Christian church— *Hallelujah hallelujah. Waheguru Ji,
please don't fail me*. It was the first time I saw religion.
Day 7: We started school. Mannu, Dev and Anshi were
in elementary. It was my first time being the *new girl*.
Everyone seemed to like me— I hadn't felt that much

kindness in days. I had a long walk to and from Solano Middle. Unfortunately, I didn't get lost.

Day 8: I got scolded for taking chocolates that were hidden in the pantry since Halloween. I was starving. I figured no one would eat them. It was January. I put them back.

Day 9: I had ten dollars in my hello kitty wallet. I didn't know when or if. I'd ever see her again. But I couldn't wait to give Mummy Ji the hair curler I had bought for her.

Day 10: The foster father sat across from me. Regarding the trauma that occurred with Mannu and I, a question escaped from his mouth. *Do you think he practiced on them?* Foster mother looked at me. She was just as dumbstruck as I. *I don't know.* She said. Till this day. I wonder. Why I didn't light the house on fire.

Awkward glances were exchanged
At each session
Along with the awkward silences
I dreaded 3:00pm every Monday
For six months
How does that make you feel
The haunting question I could not answer
Show me on this picture, where he touched you
It was a doodle of a little girl
Without descriptive body parts
I didn't know where to point
How far
How deep
Tears rushed down my face
I could not wait for the hour to end
I scribbled pictures when I was asked to
Saying anything to finish the session
Hoping six months would end soon
When did all of this start happening
Did you try stopping it
What made him touch you
The words I couldn't speak
Were counted
With each second
Ticking on the clock
The trauma wasn't my fault
Or maybe it was
Since I was the one
Being blamed

— *theRAPIST*

At least you weren't raped
Slipped from your mouth
When I told you about
Being molested
For six years
I think that statement
Is far more
Traumatic
Than the sexual abuse
I experienced

— *Invalidation*

*They enjoyed it— of course they waited to tell after all
these years!*
'Cause when you're five years old
You're euphoric at being fondled with
And when you're eight
You try telling your mom something is wrong
With the way you've been touched
But you have no words
Because
How are you supposed to know?
So you stay quiet until you're eleven
When enough is enough
There's a loss of innocence
You've grown up too quickly
You have found the words.
To explain.
How many cases are left untold?
How many cases come out, when people grow old?
I waited all of those years because I enjoyed
Being abused
How could you even think that
When you had a daughter, too?

— *Words From My Ex Best Friend's Mom*

Mummy Ji blaming herself
Left me numb
No one was there for her
When she was raped every night
For a year
Having to swallow her words
Being told to shut up
Her whole life she made a promise
To herself
She'd protect her children
Since everyone failed to keep her safe
Only to find
That the one thing that triggered her flashbacks and
Bad memories
The one thing she wanted to save us from
The one thing that happened to her
Happened to three of her children too..
She blamed herself
For what happened to us
Believing she was a bad mother
Unable to forgive herself
I blamed myself too
Not just for having gone through abuse
But for having to put Mummy Ji through it too

— *Victims Take the Pain, Shame, and the Blame*

There is a special place in hell
For those who abuse children
And a worse place for those who
Support the abusers

I think the reason I am unaffectionate
Towards family members
Yet affectionate
Towards friends and strangers
Is 'cause
I am scarred
From years of being touched by
Someone who was supposed to be
A second father

— PTSD

What's wrong
He asks
I respond with nothing
He asks
If I will ever be okay
I look at him
He sees right through me
Overlooking the blood and tears
Ignoring the war
That was fought inside of me
I tell him
I am okay

— *Overlooked*

We drank boiled sink water for days in a row
Whenever we were hungry or thirsty
I made $400 a month
Mummy Ji was overseas for six months
I was eighteen
I was the oldest
I was terrified
It was our first time alone
I remember the nights when
More water came out from my eyes
Than I had to drink that day
I tried to quiet the rumbling in my stomach
During school and work
Until the rumbling eventually stopped on its own
I couldn't look at my siblings
Without wondering how long it would be
Until we could eat again
Bread and peanut butter were familiar to us
Biweekly when I received my check
But the bread would disappear after three days
And boiled water rushed down our throats once again
Spoons went into the peanut butter jar
Can you imagine how sick I am
Of peanut butter
At this point

— *184 days*

I am a walking contradiction
Wanting to die
But looking at all of the reasons
As to why
I shouldn't

Pieces of me are taken
One by one
From everyone who fails to ask me
If I need any pieces
For myself
I continue to do an injustice to myself
When I put others first
With passion in my heart
As if these people appreciated me
As if they weren't angry
Expecting more
Mummy Ji always told me
I have so much to offer
But I don't have to give my all
To people who aren't worthy
What I didn't understand from that lesson was
That I, too
Was worthy
That I, still
Am worthy

— *I Am Not a Puzzle*

This past year
Consisted of
Coming across boys
Who faked being men
While quickly revealing
Who they were
'Cause of how they reacted to
A woman showing no interest in them

When your heart
Fails to decide
If enough is enough
You experience
One of the most
Painful
And simultaneously painless
States
As a human being—
Being numb

— *Paralyzed*

I used to confuse
Being alone
With loneliness
I was deeply
Mistaken
Being alone
Is the only
Place
That gives me
Eternal solace

Why do our brains
Blur our first years with
Our mothers
As if those years
Aren't worth remembering
As if they aren't precious
Her body fed me
Sheltered me
Kept me warm
She didn't just carry me
For seven months
She was my first home
She was the air inside my lungs
How can I ever repay
Her
Infinite lifetimes
Aren't enough

— *My First Home*

My father left and returned
Without saying goodbye
He surprised us without welcoming hellos
Perhaps that's why I linger
More often than I should
My father never had the words to express his anger
And where there's anger
There's danger
He's where I get my rage from
When the only father figure you've had
Is the woman who birthed you
You wonder why single moms are a norm
While single dads are seen as heroes
Why single mothers are underserved
While biological fathers remain strangers
He still doesn't know my favorite color
Neither do I know his, is he really my father?
When other dads showed up to class for Father's day
You wondered
What your mother did to wrong him
Since she's the one who showed up
Or if you're the one at fault
Since he didn't see your worth
They're not my kids, let's take a DNA test to prove it
No DNA test is needed for someone who is dead
Remind me again
Why I ever
Called you dad

— *No Father Figure*

I gave up on dads
When the one who was supposed to be
Mine
Supported my abuser

The foster home
Reinforced my belief
That labels
Really are just that
Labels
Regardless of who claims to be
Your mother or your
Father

The way I am able to
Feel vibes deeply
Makes me feel like a goddess and
Simultaneously uncomfortable
I am able to tell off the bat
Who will stay
Who will not
What bothers me is those who
Overestimate their stay
Put up a facade
As if I don't already know
Their intentions
It's crystal clear to me
From the start
Even when their hearts aren't

— *Energy*

We come into this world
Naked
We also leave
Naked
And in between
We don't mind the physical undressing
Of one another
But we damn do mind
Stripping our souls
To each other

A man who wants you
Does not always respect you
You will know this
Based on
How he handles
Rejection

When he calls you a
Prude
Remember that
You were not made to
Be a filling
For those who are empty
Remember that
You don't need an explanation
When you say no
Remember that
Humans can connect
In more intimate ways
Than sex
And your body isn't
His choice to make

I was
Kicking my feet
In the middle
Of the ocean
And you were
Still wondering
If you should
Dip your toes in

— *Drowning For You*

I listened to your purpose
Whenever I laid my head
On your chest
It made me realize
We're all here
For reasons
Beyond our understanding

— *Your Heartbeat*

I knew I loved you when
All I ever
Asked for
Was your time

I thought loving you
Meant that
I was excused from
Not loving myself

Sometimes I think of the things
That made me fall in love with you
The way you'd tell your jokes
And laugh
Then look over at me to see
If I was laughing too
I always thought your jokes were cheesy
But I'd laugh at the fact that
You thought they were funny
Or how you'd look shy right before eating
Preparing for the picture I was going to take
Of you
How you'd pull my cheeks
And kiss them
Following my forehead
Then my lips
Like my face was a cross
And you had just prayed
How you'd get quiet when you were sad
Hopeless when you were frustrated
Quirky when you were happy
How I was there for you during tough times
But we still could not last

I changed myself
Reshaped myself
Shrunk myself
To fit into your life
Only to find that
I never had a
Place in it
To begin with

You said I had settled for you
It took me a long time
To figure out
You were right

They say to never bring up
The mistake
Once you've forgiven someone
For it
What they failed to mention is
Hearing sorry
From someone who does the same thing
Over and over
And forgiving them for it
'Cause you expect a different result
Is insanity

— *Three Years of Apologies*

I thought
Ending it with you
Meant that
I left you
Before you could leave me
But I now know that
You left me
Before I ever realized
And I was just
Catching up

— *Closure*

I ask you to come meet me
Even though we're no longer
Together
You eagerly say yes
Even stating you'll meet me closer
To my home
As if you're subconsciously
Hoping
There's another chance
And ignoring why I ended
The relationship in the first place
I only called to return the gifts
That would otherwise end up
In the trash bin
Where they ultimately ended up
Anyway
Just like us and the relationship

I used to question
Why you jumped ship and
Left me there
To sink
You forgot
Between you and I
I'm the one who knows
How to swim

You became distant
Every time I tried to get
Closer
I stopped walking towards the road
That I thought would
Lead me to you
I paved my own path
Walked along
Added to the distance
Till you became nothing
But a memory

I wrote to you for three years
You wrote back once
For some insane reason
I thought that was enough

The fact that you thought. That you hoped. We still had a chance in the future makes me furious. When you had me in the present. The chance was given to you. So was a second. A third. For three years chances were handed to you. That our paths could cross in the future doesn't change the fact that you were unable to love me in the past. It disgusts me. That you feel you deserve another one somewhere down the line. When you couldn't do a single thing about the one. That was in front of you.

— *Wrong Timing Doesn't Exist*

It was numbing
Almost like I had taken pain killers
For emotions
But the hurt came periodically
In waves
Waves that reached the heights of
Tsunamis
Waves that never let you forget.
The hurting.
Waves that rushed in but slipped through
Every crack in your body
Waves that left you feeling
Dizzy
If you watched them for too long
Waves that consumed you
When you forgot that you were watching
Waves that tasted like the salt water
On your pillowcase
Every night
For a year

— *Breaking Up For The Last Time*

Sometimes I want to talk to me
As a child
And tell her
It will be okay
Yes, you will cry
You will get your heart broken
You will go through tragedies
You will hate yourself
People will hate you
People will talk about you
You will want to end your life several times
But you won't go through with it
'Cause you know there's another day
It may be worse than the previous one
Or it may not be
But it does get better
It always does
Everything gets worse before it gets better
But you will never see it get better
If you don't continue the journey

— *Words To My Younger Self*

It is easy to tell ourselves
We will never settle for less
As women
But when the situation arises
Most of us do
We shrink ourselves
To fit in
To find a place
We attempt to make room for ourselves
In a place that doesn't exist for us
Until we realize what we're doing
We remind ourselves
We'd never do this for a man
So why did we
Why did we
Why did we

A couple of years ago
You texted me *Happy Birthday*
In that message you mentioned
People take me for granted
You didn't list yourself
As one of those people

They tell you to find
Your talent
Your passion
Your drive
Yet for years I didn't know
Where to look
Till I stopped looking
It came to me, finally
Through a heartbreak
Through a soul shatter
Through you

— *Beautiful Beginnings*

It takes strength to leave
It takes courage to accept the relationship
Will no longer work
Yet those of us who take the step to go
Are the ones perceived as being the
Culprits

My siblings ask me
Out of joy
If I think you read my writing
I casually respond
But of course
If anyone knows you well enough
You've always kept up with
What I do
I know it brings you great pleasure
To know that I write about you
I wonder how many truths
You've discovered
About yourself

— *Through My Writing*

Sometimes the ending
Happens abruptly
Sometimes the closure
Doesn't come with forgiveness
Sometimes there is no closure
So we carry this baggage
For days, months, years on end
Forgetting that
We have the power to forgive ourselves
If we weren't forgiven
We have the power to let go of
Any guilt we placed on ourselves
We have the power to be more than
What the situation is
What the situation was
Whatever the case may be
We hold the power
To grow from the lesson
Or to dwell in the past and
Remain stagnant

Despite what they tell you
Being sensitive
Is a strength
A blessing
And a step towards a
Conscious revolution

Don't tell me there are limits
When whole books have
Been written
From 26 letters
Of the
English alphabet

We are created through sex
An art form
A connection beyond the physical
A merging of two bodies
Yet the social construct of virginity
And my past traumatic experiences
Made me feel ashamed of an act
As natural as sex
For 24 years

What is it called
When you feel so far away
From yourself
You can't find your way back
You don't recognize the person that
You see in the mirror
So you start making room for this
New person
'Cause you're unsure if
You will
Come back
To yourself

— *Dissociation*

Every person has been
To a place
Every place
Has a story

My father was
The first man
To break my heart
I feel indifferent towards
Any boy
Who comes afterwards
To do the same

I don't know what it means
To be sane
The line between sanity
And insanity is
Fragile
Just ask our politicians
They would know

— *Politics*

It brings me great sadness
To know that
I have seen more places
In the world
Than Mummy Ji has
It brings me great wisdom
To know
She has seen more worlds
Through her children
That I have
Yet to understand

— *Perspective*

The moon sends me messages
Every night
She pulls the tides with the same gravity
That keeps me from drowning in you
The moon reminds me every night
That I am full
Like her
Radiating light and mystery
When I go through my phases
The moon is waiting for me
To howl for you
She has listened to the conversations
I've had about you
She keeps them a secret
When she goes into crescent
The moon lights up the sky
During her nightly presence
Never bothered by who notices
And who doesn't

— *Moon Messages*

When you look for happiness
Outside of yourself
You're a prisoner
Trapped on the outside
Desperately looking for a way in
When turning inward
Should have been done
In the first place

I know it isn't fair
When you can't decide if
You should give a situation
A shot or not
You've been taught to live life
To go with the flow
To see what happens
To take the risk
But you don't have to take
Every chance
Disguised as an opportunity
To live

Love is the
Essence
Of the universe

People ask me what my greatest fear is
Sure I'm scared of spiders
Heights
Snakes
The normal fears we all have
But none of these will ever equate to
My greatest fear of not living up to
My potential
That I still have leftover talent
I haven't tapped into in my last moments
Will be my biggest regret
So I try every day
Every single day
To figure out a new part of myself
Artistically
Scientifically
Spiritually
To learn myself
Who I am
In depth
To make sure
I'm not holding back on myself
I can't have the universe be upset with me
When we meet again
I don't want to be mad at myself
For not living passionately

— *My Greatest Fear*

Teach someone to appreciate alone time
And they will show you
How well they learned
By no longer depending on your company

— Lessons My Sister Learned From Me

I have always questioned if everything I have thought is really mine. Is this thought my own? I cannot say whose it is; my mother's or my father's? My teachers? My siblings, friends, past lover? Perhaps society? No one has asked me what I have thought about anything, before putting an idea into my brain. Is my thought process mine— or has it been constructed by the various minds I have come across? For the first thought ever formed was probably created through a crashing of nebulas, a cluster of stars, colliding galaxies. Do we think because it's instinct? To survive? Is it something we learn? Some of us don't think at all.

— *Questions*

When a man tells you
That you're different from other girls
He fails to realize
That is not a compliment
Or perhaps it is his way of
Starting a war inside of you
Against yourself
For who am I to compete with
My sisters
Who am I to take part in a war
That continues to divide us
Who am I to feel that the space I take
Is more special than that of a woman
Who is just like me
But I really want to ask
Who are you
To tell me
I am different from my sisters
When I never signed up
For this competition

It's crazy how most of us
Don't realize
We've dated misogynists
Until we're no longer with them

— *Love Really Is Blind*

Half love
Half effort
Half heartedly
I refuse to believe we have
Another half
Or a *better half*
Or a half that makes us whole
For what is missing outside of me?
Who told you, you aren't whole?
Half of anything leaves me empty
I am still recovering from the half love
That poisoned me

— *Two Halves Make A "Hole" In Your Heart*

You wouldn't have to
Beg
If he stayed for your
Soul
Instead of
Your body

Why do men find it necessary
To base a woman's worth
On other men's opinions of her
Why do men automatically assume
They know a woman
'Cause of what is said about her
As if rumors are the foundation
Of who a woman is
'Cause it's crazy how locker room talk
Now takes place
In group chats

— *With Men As The Admins*

When he asks you
Why it happened
Instead of asking you
If you're okay
He is not
On your side

I often ignore
Men's opinions on what I should do
Regarding my physical appearance
If I should remove the hair on my body or not
They don't understand that their opinions go through
One ear
And out the other
What concerns me is when
Women find the need to tell me what to do
With my body as well
As if we aren't controlled enough
By a patriarchal society
Some women
Fall into that category of control
Brainwashed
I hate when women participate in no shave November
Made me cover my legs in shame
I am not concerned about
Whether a woman chooses to
Remove the hair on her body or not
I'm with you if you do
I'm with you if you don't
She's been around all of the guys
Makes me feel ashamed for the women
Who allow these thoughts to form into words
Regarding one of my sisters
While ignoring the men
Who have *been around all of the girls*
We don't need any more people
Trying to police our bodies

— *Internalized Misogyny*

Repetitive cycles of explaining yourself
To those who don't care to
Understand you
Is what insanity looks like

Discounted school lunches
Waived college app fees
Low income apartments
Brown skin
A history of hardships
You're so lucky
They tell me
For being a low income student
For having a difficult past
For being Brown 'cause I supposedly have more options
That whatever I have achieved is
Purely out of luck
Not hard work
Negating the fact that people of color
Have their potential questioned
At one point or another
Not that I am ungrateful for being Brown
But it's as if being Brown is something I chose to be
That being poor makes me lucky 'cause
I get a few fees waived here and there
I don't know why any of these things
Make me lucky
Since I did not choose to be Brown
Or poor
Or someone with a rough past
So when you tell me I am lucky to be these things
I have no idea what you mean
When the massacres of my people
Show otherwise
When my own upbringing
Shows otherwise

A woman has been taught
To demand respect
She has to earn it
A man has respect
Before he even speaks

I find it amusing
How offended men get
When you make it a point
That you don't need them
'Cause some of them don't stop
Begging
For a chance
Our no's are responded to
With more questions or catcalls
Several insults
Even death threats
It is scary seeing a man
Having a tantrum over not having control
Of a woman
It is more terrifying to read about my sisters
Being killed
For saying no

— *But We're The Crazy Ones*

Why is my mom a prostitute
For getting divorced
After being a mother of four
With a man who decided we weren't his
Why is my single mother *the prostitute*
When the one who entered her home
To have us
Couldn't take responsibility for his children

— *Hypocrisy*

They'd rather you keep quiet
About the rape
For old reputation's
Sake

— *Disservice*

You throw like a girl
Perhaps because I am a girl
You fight like a girl
I have heard that statement far too many times
Being said to men
'Cause being a woman creates these assumptions
That I am somehow the weaker sex
Or men referred to as being feminine
Is the equivalent to being a *fag*
When your mother felt like 20 bones in her body
Were simultaneously breaking to get you here
Did you forget that you are partly woman?
Your clitoris enlarged to a penis
So there really is no difference
Between you and I
Yet there's still an emphasis
That men are the stronger sex
Isn't it the weak who need reassurance?
Now somehow being kicked in the scrotum
Is a comparison to giving birth
Who the hell made that one up?
Delusions are masked through taking medications
But there's no cure for the male population
Besides teaching our men to be less ignorant
That was a pussy ass punch
I won't forget that one
But fortunately, for you
I took it as a compliment

— *feMENism*

Working days and nights concurrently
Taught me
Even wanting financial stability
Is a form of servitude
Due to corporate greed
Trading in my time and sleep
Didn't give me financial stability
And it still took away
My mental ease

I think what makes me most melancholic
Is feeling like I don't belong here
Not in this universe
Or dimension
Or this place in time
Not in this world
Not to anyone
Not even to myself

Sometimes I wonder if
My low self-esteem is the result of
Years of sexual abuse
From a relative
Years of name calling and insults
From family friends and grandparents
Or if ultimately
It is only my fault
I am like this

I am exhausted from hearing people tell me
I need a man
To make me happy
I need a man
To take care of me
I need a man
To make my life full
I want a man
But I sure as hell don't need one
I went without a man my whole life
So if my past relationship counts
As me having a man
Then the definition of what a man is
Should be changed
'Cause I've made it this far
Without one
Because I don't need any more people telling me
Who and what I need
Because I already have everything I need
Within me
Because wanting a man
Wanting.
Is a whole different thing

It doesn't matter how much he says he loves you
If he isn't willing to meet you halfway
Words show nothing
Actions can't be fully trusted
Consistency is the key
It is not difficult
To put in effort
For someone you claim
You love

— *Lazy Boys, Stop Wasting Our Time*

The men who say they care about
Gender equality
Don't know the first thing
About equality
When they hesitate to call themselves
Feminists

— *Masculinity So Fragile*

I've been feeling this void
That people
Places
Things
Don't seem to fill
It's expanding as I search for
The missing piece
To seal this gap
Something I have yet
To lay my finger on
Experience
Or feel
To get rid of this emptiness

My horoscope sign
Is a constant reminder
That I am always searching
For balance
Yet when it comes to
Emotions
I never did well
In grey areas

— *Libra*

I am usually referred to as being friendly
Or approachable
Someone who gets along with most people
Often and well
But I've always been a bit of a loner
In the seventh grade
My friends had a different lunch period from mine
So I stayed in the courtyard
Observing
Eating
Reading books
Lost in imaginative worlds making my own connections
The students in my classes used to
Call me a nerd
Or weird
But it didn't bother me
I never felt the need to surround myself with
Superficial friendships
To avoid being alone
If there's one thing I'm proud of about myself
It's that I learned how precious
Solitude is
At a young age

— *Loner*

Owe is one letter away from
Being own
It's why I believe
I don't owe anyone
Anything
And no one owes me anything
I am my own world
I owe myself the world

To feel pain
Is to know you're alive

Men often forget
Don't they
How much we sacrifice as women
When we give them more than
What we receive
How we put their happiness
Above ours
How we leave our homes
And enter theirs
Putting our lives behind us
Starting a new chapter
Like it was nothing

My heart can no longer tolerate
The burdens of those
Who don't belong
Alongside of me

For you to minimize
Your own pain
In comparison to what
Others have gone through
That you have not
Is self harm
For someone to minimize your pain
Regarding any situation
Regarding what they did to you
That you shouldn't feel a certain way
Is abuse

— *Your Feelings Are Legitimate*

I had grown tired
From being genuine with others
I put up a wall between
Myself and the world
Only causing myself to greatly suffer
And learning that was not
The answer

— Don't Lose Your Authenticity Because Of Others

We love
We love
We make love
But I am still not
Cured

Leading someone on
Is such a misused phrase
What does it mean
To lead someone on
When you never showed them
Any mutual feelings of interest
In the first place
Why is my kindness mistaken for me
Wanting to go to first, second or third base
Why do my manners so often
Get confused for flirtation
'Cause I don't see women looking me up and down
When I treat them warmly
I am starting to believe
It's another phrase
Made up by men
Who are simply too fragile
To handle rejection
That they need to put the blame
On a woman
Another reason for men to make themselves
Feel worthy and validated
Just another *nice guy*
Who *finished last* after having a tantrum
A whiny man who got
Friend zoned
'Cause he didn't understand *no*
So he came up with
Yet another term
To point his finger
At a woman

The prefix in the word
Menstruation
Must explain why we feel
Tremendous pain as women
When we shed away
Our nutrients
Our materials
Our blood
The home within us
Gets destroyed every month
Yet men still try to keep power over
The functioning of our bodies
As if we are their property
As if they have a womb to know what it's like
As if they'd ever allow us to control the blood they shed
In wars
Throughout the world

For years
I was taught
Being angry
Is wrong
Ugly
Unfeminine
So I masked that anger into
Other feelings
Sadness, disappointment, frustration
Anxiety, confusion, voicelessness
Dissociation from my true feelings
Anything but anger 'cause
I was told not to be furious
Just to be pleasing to the male species
By suppressing my feelings
You'd think I'd have mastered it by now
Yet after all of these years
I feel nothing but
Rage

— *You're Allowed To Feel Every Emotion Across The Spectrum*

Before trying to apologize to someone
When you want to say no
Ask yourself
Why
They require an apology
Or explanation

Forced conversations have a way
Of making me feel like I lack social skills
When that isn't true
We're not meant to vibe with everyone
Even with people we've known for years
We may have nothing more than small talk
Then there are those who make you feel like
You've known them from a past life
'Cause you're able to talk about anything
Or nothing
And still enjoy the silence together

— *My Thoughts On Small Talk*

I give people countless opportunities
To be honest with me
To share their feelings
To tell me if I have wronged them
So when they hesitate
Become distant
Or hold things in
I do the same
When they ask me why I feel a certain way
I leave them hanging
'Cause I am not wasting my time
Being transparent
When someone else is being vague
I am no longer exerting any energy
Being open with someone
When I can't receive the same respect
Honesty and closeness
In return

I suppose I majored in psychology
To figure out
What kind of crazy
I am

Maybe my father thought
Bribing was a way to show us love
Perhaps 'cause his parents used this tactic on him
Still it was never effective with us
I always felt shameful and insulted when he did this
'Cause all we ever wanted
Was for him to be there for us and for our mother
And it's because of my father
That I've never found peace in material things
And it's because of my father
That I never will

The only reason men have
Constantly oppressed women
In history
In the present
At all
Is 'cause they're afraid of us
They're afraid that we'll excel
Be better than them at
Everything they do
Except we do everything
When we're menstruating
When we're pregnant
While we're taking care of children and our homes
While being underestimated
While dealing with sexist remarks
While dealing with misogyny
While dealing with sexual harassment
I can go on
'Cause even then
We still do whatever it is
With grit
And that's too much for the male species
To handle

I have yet to meet a man
Who would leave his home
To live with his wife's family
After marriage

— *Double Standards*

When I am telling someone my story
I sometimes fail to distinguish
If they are actively listening without judgement
Or drawing conclusions
About me
From their level of perception

It's shocking to know
How many people perceive me as someone who
Lacks depth
Simply because I laugh a lot
I am sorry that humor
Has always been my defense mechanism
To be frank, I am not sorry at all
'Cause I am not waiting around
For anyone's approval
But I am sorry
That your poor judgment
Caused you to miss out on
Knowing someone
Like me

— *Not My Loss*

It is not your fault
When your mother came here
Forced to bring your father
With her
It is not your fault
When your father leaves the home
Without you
Without your mother
Without words
For so long
You may have been the glue that
Kept them together
It doesn't always keep things
Stable
It doesn't always keep things
Inseparable
Still, your job isn't
To be the glue

— *Arranged Marriage and Divorce*

Do you see why I did that?
Do you see where I'm coming from?
Of course
I always do
Do most people see where I'm coming from?
No
But they expect me to see life
From their view
As if there aren't different angles
To the truth

— *One Sided Empathy*

Having heart to hearts
With the wrong people
Will leave you
Heartbroken
Why if
You're the only one
With the
Heart

Just like loving someone
From a distance
You can miss someone
Without wanting them in your life

When I've hit past
The lowest of lows
Thinking it couldn't possibly get
Any worse
I think of reaching out to you
Mentally and emotionally regressing
To a time where I was used to
This type of hurt
This type of numbness
This familiar feeling that I would
Never be okay
Dwelling in despair
Almost sending that text message
Till I remind myself
I will only feel
Emptier
Than I already do

— *Past Rock Bottom*

Vulnerability is precious
You risk being
Open and aware that you
Could be hurt
You also risk being
Receptive to falling in love
It is still the most real thing
A raw thing
To be able to show a part of yourself
Who you are
How you feel
Something most would consider
Weak
Is the strongest thing you can do for yourself
'Cause to love
To care
Takes strength
It is valuable
Difficult
Seen as less than
In a world where
Coldness
Is lauded

— *Wrong Praise*

I often keep my thoughts
Contained
Inside my mind
Belly
Heart
As if my body is a basement
A storage room
Filled with vulnerabilities
Thoughts of fury
Agony and despair
That I no longer want to face
I keep them buried deep inside of me
Every now and then
I feel them creeping up
I think that's what makes me
Most dangerous

I found your cologne
In my bathroom
Wondering why
Mummy Ji got it for dad
So I sprayed it everywhere
Until the scent filled my nose
But there was no lump
In my throat this time
I was searching for inspiration
The universe gave me a smell
The one that initially
Brought me closer to you
The one that ultimately took me
To hell

— *Writer's Block*

Self-confidence was what
I lost
With you
And gained
Without you

One reason our relationship failed
Was 'cause work was more important to you
That's okay 'cause my work is important to me too
Working on my relationship with myself
Working on my relationship with my family
Working on the work that helps me grow
I understood where you were coming from
When you chose work over me
9-5 appealed to you
While inner work was my priority

The saddest part about endings with people are. Their
memories. The leftover information you have of them.
How those things don't get erased from. Your mind.
Even after people leave.

There is something so respectful
Inspiring
Majestic
About women
Who have cried their eyes out
In the public bathroom
When our lives are anything
But easy
When the world is falling apart
And yet
We are able to hold it together
Quickly wiping away the tears
Re-applying some make up
Looking in the mirror
Telling ourselves it'll be okay
Kicking the door open
Like a war didn't just take place

— *Majestic Creatures*

If I could put
This void
Into words
Perhaps it wouldn't
Stay
Any longer…

I wonder how long
I've been sad
Lonely
Depressed
Before becoming aware of it

— *Days Have Become Years*

Let's touch each other
Without uttering a
Word
Then you'll know
Exactly
What I'm feeling

He stays in my head
With no intent of
Paying rent
He moves to my heart
When he wants me to
Create art
For him

— *Overstaying His Visit*

I uttered a few lines
As a mischievous response
To his comment regarding softness
To which he asked
Where'd you get that?
To which I replied
I wrote it

— *One Of The Best Indirect Compliments I've Received
For My Writing*

75% of earth's body is controlled
By the moon
I always found it a coincidence
That humans are 75% water
Too
If the moon can control
The ocean
Undoubtedly
She controls our
Emotions

Ritu means all seasons
Maybe that's why
My mood changes
Are frequent

A sister is. A friend. An occasional nuisance. A partner in life's journey. Someone who will make you angry one minute and say sorry the next. A sister is someone who understands you. Without words. An additional soul mate. So I must have done good deeds in past lives. To be one. And much greater deeds than that. To have one.

— *To Anshi*

I always thought there was
Something wrong with me
'Cause of how often
People would come in
And out of
My life
I've learned throughout the years
Most people are temporary
Those who were for me
And the one I've been for others

The freedom Mummy Ji hoped for
After getting married
Did not come
Yet relatives tell me
My dreams of traveling and being happy
Will come true
Once I am married to a man
As if I can't make these things happen
On my own
As if I haven't already started working towards
My dreams
As if I've ever needed a man
To do anything for me
As if my happiness is in the hands of anyone
Other than myself

— *I Am A Rich Man*

My mother has passed down
Her traits of being
Lively
Sarcastic
Gentle
But mostly
She and I share the experience of
Having grown up too quickly

— *What The Abuse Does To You*

I wonder how much
Mother Earth
Would flourish
If humans weren't here
I wonder how many
Heartbreaks
We've caused her
How much self-hatred
She has had to deal with
Because of us
If she blames herself for what is happening
If she thinks she is ugly because of
How much we change her
By destroying forests
Water
Life
Killing each other
I wonder if she has ever wanted
An asteroid to hit her
If she, too, has ever felt
Like she should
Die
To end all of the pain

The ocean has kicked my ass
Several times
But I still cannot find myself
Angry with it

— *The Anger Resonates With Me*

Countless times
I've been told to see a shrink
But when you're in something
Too deep
You begin to understand
That superficial people
Don't see your beginning
And can't come close to seeing
Your end
They stay on the surface
Not knowing what depth is
Concluding
There is something
Wrong with you
That
You're crazy

— But You're Not

The only image of my dad
That has stayed in my head
Is the one of him leaving
His back to my face

Half truths
Are still lies

You hear about your neighbor's husband
Coming home late
Missed calls
So many missed calls
She's worried
She knocks on your door to ask if you've seen him
You tell her you did, earlier that week at the store
Purchasing a bouquet of flowers
To which she says she didn't receive
But he's your neighbor
He still greets you the same way as he passes by
Smiling
Offering you treats
Why should you see him differently
He hasn't done anything wrong to you
You still get a weird feeling in your stomach
Uneasiness
A hint of betrayal
You hear about it all of the time
You think you're immune to it
Now it's fifteen years later
You still feel like it won't happen to you
It can't
Until the late nights come
And the missed calls
Those damn, missed calls
Excuses for every feeling in your gut
Justification for every question you bring up
Except the one question
Which keeps you up every night
Why wasn't I enough

— *Infidelity*

He told me no one would ever love me

He told me no one would ever love me
The way he has
That no one could love me as much as
He loves me
But how silly of him to think that way
While hurting me
While being aware of what he was doing
And still going along with his actions
As if he wasn't going to get caught
How hypocritical of him to say that no one
Could love me as much as he does if he ever did
As if I'm unlovable
As if no one else will see me in the light
Or in a better light
'Cause if he truly loved me
Why would he let me slip through his fingers
Just to say he'll always see me as
The one who got away

Always go with your gut
It'll save you a lot of time
And pain
In the long run

I sit here
Pondering
About the apologies
That will never come
I also sit here
Pondering
About the apologies
I gave
When it wasn't my fault

There was a spark
Between us
A current that started
In you
And ended in me
I wish one of us would have mentioned
The electricity

— *Lost Connection*

You make me feel every emotion
To its full potential

— *Happiness, Sadness... Love*

Do you know how many times
I had to stop myself
From dialing your number
Just so I could hear
Your voice

— *When It's Over*

When you fail to make a decision
When you choose to be passive
Either life or another person
Will decide something for you
Being inactive towards making a decision
Is still a step towards ultimately making a decision
'Cause neglecting to decide on something
Will still end in some way
You can't leave your life
Or anyone else's life on standby

Most of us have parents who give us so much
So much that we cannot repay them for in this life
Or any life for that matter
Our parents bring us into this world
They support us with whatever they have
They instill values and beliefs in us
But we don't always have to agree with their thinking
We don't always have to believe
What they were brought up with
We have our own minds
Our own experiences that may have
Shaped us a bit differently from them
And because of this
I may not always agree with my mother or my stepfather
But that doesn't mean I love them any less
'Cause I do appreciate everything they have done for me
But I have this one life and I don't know how long it is
And although I'm in debt to my parents
For what they have provided for me
I am not required to believe what they believe
I am not required to give them my life
In exchange
For their sacrifices
'Cause I didn't ask to be here
I was brought here
And I deserve to have the freedom
Of making my own choices

— *Not Selfish, I Am My Own Essence*

People are quick to
Complicate
The simplest of things
If only they saw
How exhausting
It is

Being happy 10 days in a row
Does not mean
The sadness left
If you're happy 10 days
Out of 30
120 days
Out of 365
The depression
Is not gone

— *More Than A State Of Mind*

Having to choose between dealing with
Depression or anxiety
When both hit you at once
Is like living in a mental paradox

— *The Battle*

Yes, be authentic with people
Be real
But please understand that
Being real doesn't mean
Giving your all to everyone
That will leave you empty
When you continue to give
You leave no room to receive
Be truthful, honest, genuine
With everyone
But only give to the few
Who value you

What I've noticed about
Imitation in art
Is people expect you
To be okay with
Getting inspired by you
Without giving you
Credit
For being the inspiration

— *Imitation Is Not A Compliment*

Too many of us are afraid of
What others think of us
We keep others in our lives
By continuing to follow them
On social media to avoid drama
While going against our gut feelings
Adding toxicity to our lives
'Cause we remain fearful of
Someone's perception of us
Rolling our eyes whenever we come across
A person's picture or status update
Resenting ever befriending them to begin with
But I'm here to tell you not to be afraid
To remove yourself
From people
Situations
Social media
That no longer impact you positively
Unfollow
Unfriend
Delete
Even if that person is me
You owe yourself that much liberty

— *No Explanations Needed*

Aren't you tired
Of carrying
Those
Burdens
In your heart

— *To The Men Who Keep Quiet*

There's been a fight
One that the neighbors didn't hear this time
But you swear you'll never call him again
You're done
A couple of days go by
He calls to apologize for hurting you
He doesn't know what took over him
You take him back without hesitation
He's a bit sweeter now
He brings groceries home out of guilt
He's happy to see you
You believe things are different this time around
You're cooking dinner
He's pouring wine into a glass that seems endless
He puts the glass away
Grabs the whole bottle instead
Like he always does after a long day
But these long days don't end up with you two
On the couch in front of the television
They don't take you to the bedroom
For drunk lovemaking
No, these long days end up with fists in your face
A black eye
Weeping on the shower floor
After the wine bottle ends up broken in your hands
You swear you'll never call him again
You're done
A couple of days go by
He calls to apologize for hurting you
He doesn't know what took over him
You....

I know too many sisters
Who have kept quiet
About the abuse they've faced
This does not
Go against
Feminism
This does not
Make any of these women
Cowards
Survivors of abuse
Deserve peace
And they deserve to get that peace
In their own way
Whether or not
They report the abuse
Or choose to remain silent

Grow through
What you go through
Glow through
What you go through
Grow and glow
Grow and glow
Grow and glow

The gap between life and death
Is nothing short of an education
As a human being

My brothers have been
The only consistent
Men
In my life
How lucky must I be
To have that kind of love
Treasure
Protection
The kind of feelings you experience
Through bonding with
Brothers
Is a blessing
To be a sister to my brothers
Is something I'll forever cherish
In this lifetime
And hopefully my next

— *Strong Men*

I have never asked my mother
If she has become tired of
Being my father
Too

— *Not Her Job*

What happens when my
Brothers
Sister
And I
Lose our mother tongue
What happens when we contribute
To the very western colonization
That aimed to destroy our culture
What happens when we speak English
As if it was our native language to begin with
Yet we forget how to greet
Our elders
Our roots
Our beginning
Our home
Does this also make us
Murderers

— *Maa Boli (Mother Tongue)*

Being proud or ashamed of
Being born into
A certain caste
A certain class
A certain status
Is what continues this emphasis
On discrimination
Along with the ignorance and the shaming
It's what adds onto this presumption
Of upholding a certain reputation
Behind a tradition
That has been outdated
Since the day it was created

— *Leave The Caste In The Past*

Mentioning that I am not interested
When a man tries to talk to me
Doesn't usually work
And why not
Why does it not
Any decent human being would understand
A woman's choice
However
Many men think you need them
Many men think no means yes
'Cause having a boyfriend
Is more powerful than saying
I'm not interested
It implies I would be interested
If I wasn't already with a man
So remind me again
How men are able to handle
Rejection
Remind me again why
Another man claiming I'm his
Is more respected
Than my disinterest

— *The Stigma Behind: I Have A Boyfriend*

It's my fault
It's my fault
It's my fault
I tell the therapist

— *On Being Sexually Abused For Six Years*

I primarily experience the world
Through my emotions
Feeling immensely about most people
Places
And situations
Around me
It's about attention to detail
For a full experience
When others do not
Feel as deeply
About similar events
There's a loss of connection
Which tends to make this trait
A strength
Just as much of a
Challenge

— *Deep Thinker*

Feminine energy is so divine
Why do you think
Women find it difficult
To forgive each other
We touch each other in places
Men don't even know
Exist

You wait and you
Wait
And the message
Finally arrives

— *Silence Is A Message Too*

Ritu Kaur

I've had deeper conversations
Through my eyes
And through touch
Than any words I have ever
Listened to
Or spoken
To anyone

— *Body Language*

I looked at him
The same way
I look at
Stars

Smell is the sense that produces
The most vivid flashbacks
Of memories that have been long forgotten
It is the sense that tries to help us make sense
Of the scents we've acquired throughout our lives
Our minds work effortlessly to pin down the connection
Between a certain smell and a certain memory
For familiarity
For adventure
For nostalgia
For an old love

— *Olfactory*

When I feel like I am
Missing something
That Earth cannot give me
I find my answer instantly
That I just wasn't made for
This planet

— *Alien*

In an age where
My generation
Has countless options
To be who and what we desire
Most of us still feel limited
Lost
Confused
Bombarded with options
To get a higher education
To intern for free
To work in the fields we got educated in
In exchange for unlivable wages
Or to make a living out of something
That doesn't appeal to us
With added familial and societal pressure
That we should have it figured out
Constantly told to find our passion when
Schools and society did very little to nothing
To help us go that route

It's important for the
Conscious
To bring
The unconscious
To consciousness
Both in our minds
And in the masses

— *Wake Up*

Our society emphasizes
Physical well being
But forgets to mention
The other aspects of health
That need value and care just as well
For us to be the healthiest versions
Of ourselves

— *Mental Health, Emotional Health, Spiritual Health*

You learn a lot about a person
Based on what they laugh at
You understand their sense of humor
Even if you may not agree with it
You learn to distinguish between
Who is intelligent and
Who isn't

— *Sense Of Humor Taught Me*

Can you spare some change, please?
I want to ask my people
What they're willing to spare
For change
I offer food
A hug
A few bucks
Instead

— *Compassion is "Change"*

They get upset at our
Thick and detailed accents
The way we speak
English
Is an art which has
Escaped beautifully
From our lips
But I think I've pinned down
Why they become livid
At the way we speak
The richness in our history
Transfers to our tongue
Yet when they learn our languages
Us, people of color
Our languages
They're unable to speak them
Eloquently
And it makes them angry
That we're intricate
No matter what we speak
While they lack richness
Altogether

My eyes have grown tired from witnessing
The senseless acts of violence
Against my sisters and brothers
My ears have grown weary
From listening to the false promises
To bring about change
My heart feels heavy
For the mothers and fathers
Who were unaware
That was their final goodbye
To their child(ren)
If they got a farewell to begin with
My spirit weeps for the
Overwhelmingly sad state
Of the world

— *Humans But No Humanity*

I don't see bodies
I see souls
For some reason
We've become okay with
Half of the world's souls dying
From hunger and without homes
While we slave away to fund
World wars

My grandparents have been over for a month now
Nani Ji (grandmother) has a tibial fracture
She still manages to gather up enough strength
To make us a traditional snack
Nani Ji leaves the pot on the stove once it's prepared
Mummy Ji quickly fills up her own plate
Swallowing spoonfuls of her mother's treat
My mother has the talent of
Cooking just like my grandmother
I feel disheartened knowing I still haven't learned
To cook artistically like them
What breaks me most about looking at my mother
Eating her own mother's food excitedly after so long
Is the reminder that one day
I will eat food made by my mother
For the last time

Hayward is the ghetto
Usually said by those who don't know
It's the heart of the bay
It's where my heart resides
Born in Merced, California
Stayed in Hayward all my life
I could never be ashamed of
The place that brought me up
What's normal to me may be dangerous to you
What's normal to you may not be a familiar view to me
I know real danger isn't just men saggin' their pants
Danger to me isn't based on a person's accent
It isn't people covered in tattoos
Smoking joints outside their homes
Danger may be throwing up gang signs
Having a preference for a certain color
Danger is hearing shots fired
Not knowing if it's the cops or a brother
But danger isn't dependent on a brother's skin color
What the media portrays is not real danger
The real danger is the media
Constantly brain washing ya
Causing you to hate strangers
Who don't look or talk like ya
But we're all connected
We're all the same
Danger ain't these things
They put in your brain

— *Danger Has No Color*

I have noticed when people find it difficult to say my
name. I, too, have a hard time enunciating theirs. Didn't
mama teach you how to use your tongue?
But where are you really from, Suzanne?
It's Susan.
Sorry, I can't pronounce that. Do you have a nickname,
Suzanne?
Sure, it's Susie.
Sushi?
No, it's Susie. Sooozeee. She sounds it out this time,
annoyed.
Ohhh, I am sorry, Sushi, it's just that I was born in the
states and have never heard of that name.
Sushi corrects me again. I keep trying and failing. Sushi
introduces me to her daughter, Jill.
But it's hard to say Jill, so instead I call her Hell. I hope
she'll be okay with it. Actually, I don't care. Sushi's
husband, Boob walks in. He chuckles when I call him
Boob. I don't get why, that is his name.
Don't underestimate me. My tongue can slip too.

—*My Name Is Not An Inconvenience*

That needs more color, fill up all of the white space
My people of color
Find it hard to believe that statement
When our generations have faced catastrophes
For being colorful
Forced to stay small
But we are still here
Our blood has not
Spilled in vain
The universe reminds us
To expand
To add more color
To fill up the space
We will continue
To expand our existence
To add color in our homes
We will not forget to fill up
The white space
On our Earth

— *My People of Color Are Art*

They asked me
If I was poor
I told them
Only in the ways
That didn't matter

Her pink sweater was in the toilet
When I walked into the bathroom
All of the first grade girls were giggling
Trying to flush it down
I asked something along the lines of
What are you guys doing?
No answer
Again, I muttered something like
This seems wrong, why are you doing this?
One of the girls stated it was Brianna's sweater
And they were doing it because she's Black
This is wrong, stop guys. Where is Brianna?
Giggles but no response
I looked around for Brianna
She was nowhere to be found
Lunch ended and Mrs. D asked all of us first graders
Who was present during the incident
Who said anything to stop it
All of the girls said they did nothing to stop it
When it came to me, I said no as well
Not because I didn't say anything to stop it
But English isn't my first language
I was unable to comprehend and unable to explain
So trouble followed me too
I never saw Brianna in school again
I had a flashback of this event almost two decades later
Putting together what had happened
Understanding what Mrs. D had asked me
How speaking English can help you
And not knowing it cannot
But I wasn't worried about myself
I was thinking about Brianna
How she was doing
How that may not have been her first bullying experience
For being Black
And how it certainly wasn't her last

— *I Am Sorry, Brianna*

I am unsure as to who
My younger self
Would see
If she looked at me currently
If me as a child
Would now recognize me
If she'd be embarrassed at
Who I became
Or proud of who I am
If I have disappointed her
Or worse yet
Failed her
If I have hurt her
If she has wanted to hug me
Or offer words of wisdom
If she has laughed at
Parts of my life
And cried because of
Everything else

Eleven-year-old me
Can't testify alone
Nine-year-old Mannu
Can't tolerate seeing him again
The district attorney tries to help Mannu
Gain strength
Tries to help Mannu gain strength
The therapist is worried that
Mannu might lose it
She's worried that Mannu might lose it
Six years of abuse
I suffer from *six years of abuse*
Mannu can't remember
He can't remember
How many years
Of abuse
He has suffered from
How many years of abuse he has suffered from
Our case is filed together
It's filed *together*
I'm not allowed to testify for the both of us
Not allowed
To testify
For the both of us
The trial ends
It ends
The abuser's 25 year sentence
25 year sentence
Gets reduced
Reduced
To four years

— *Four Years*

My father calls a few times a year
Not on my birthday
Not on any holidays
They are usually random calls
That cause me to stare at my phone
When his name pops up on my screen
Whether it's 4am
Or 6pm
I stare until my phone has rang long enough
For me to answer with an inch of hope
That it'll be an apology for all of those years of
Mistreatment
My name's still the same
But it sounds unfamiliar when he says it
He gets straight to the point
For the reason of his phone call
And just like that
I lose hope again

— *40 Second Phone Calls*

When someone compares your problems
And pain
To starving kids
To disabled people
To how small we are in the universe
They are doing you an injustice
When it comes to life challenges
No one said life would be fair
It's important to acknowledge
We all go through something different
We all go through phases
Still, we have to deal with our issues
No matter how big or how microscopic

Isn't it strange
How the void
How the nothingness
Can feel so heavy

Bringing up your past mistakes
After accepting your apology
Is not forgiveness

It'll be okay someday, if not now
I promise
Life is trivial and simple
Humans are the ones who complicate it
There's a solution to everything
Sometimes it may take time to get to it
Sometimes it's in front of our eyes
That's when we usually tend to miss it

I want to write about everything
Since I feel everything

How can it be
His laugh
Gives me life
And takes my breath away
All at once

I wonder if there is
A person on Earth
Made specifically for me
Who will make me forget
Every bad thing that has happened to me
With his first glance

He asks me about the men who flirt with me
I purposely acknowledge them to get his attention
I noticed him eyeing you, is he trying to get to know you
He sounds insecure
I look him dead in the eye
Why do you care
He maintains eye contact
Gazes back and forth at both of my eyes a few times
Because I do, I just do
He says while caressing my arm
The liquor in me wants to speak
I calm it down
Staying quiet instead
He awaits an answer
I gather up some courage
But you've already made the decision that we can't be
I sound stern
I look at him again
Eyes hazy
He's there
In front of me
But I miss him already

I wasn't afraid of love
To love, or to be loved
I was afraid
I'd make the mistake of
Falling again
Instead of
Rising in love

I think it's a flaw in
Human understanding
How we require a beginning
How we long for an end

I am thankful for the people
Who have made it easy for me to
Cut them out of my life
They have reminded me
I am always in control of the energy
I surround myself with

It comes in waves

— *The Happiness*

Being in love feels like you can finally breathe
Not shallow breathing either
Being in love is like
Being in a meditative state 'cause you're
Content with everything around you
Long, deep breaths in between laughter
It's why you feel the air escape your lungs
If it does end up in heartbreak

You don't make me giggle
You make me laugh until my stomach is aching
Till I'm trying to catch my breath
From shedding tears of joy
You don't give me vague compliments
You tell me what you love about me
Internally and externally
With a reason behind each adjective
Till I'm smiling and shying away with
A glow from your words
You don't tell me you love me
Without following through
You show me when you put your jacket on me
Or warm up your car for me
Or when you mimic the way I talk for fun
And kiss me a million times to contain the warmth
You don't wait to answer my calls
You pick up the first heart beat
As if every call I've made to you
Gives you a sense of urgency
You don't shower me with love
You drown me in it

— *You Don't Know Balance Either*

I'm sitting at my favorite tea house
Near your home
Glancing up at the door whenever someone walks in
Hoping you'll eventually
Walk in too
To find me here
Writing about you

I think you and I both know
We were *could haves*
For each other in this life
We could have
Tried harder
We could have
Been together
We could have
Been beautiful
We *should have*
Been eternal

— *Perhaps Another Time, Life, Universe*

I know how you feel
Is an outdated
Phrase

— *Please Stop Using It*

I've been depressed for years due to several reasons
But none of these reasons have been due to my
Sexual orientation
I've felt lonely from years of being misunderstood
But I've never felt lonely due to the gender
I'm attracted towards
I've felt anxious from being dissatisfied with the way
My body looks
But I've never experienced anxiety for being born
In the wrong body
I've grown accustomed to the art of dissociation
But I will never know the tragedy of
Gender dysphoria
My brother is the strongest man I know
Not because of what he's gone through
But because he isn't afraid to be
Who he is

— *I Stand With You, LGBTQ+*

Are you Indian? You're pretty for an Indian girl
I never know if I should feel complimented
Or insulted
When I hear this
I have every right to feel confused
Even though these men may not mean to sound insulting
I still stop myself from rolling my eyes
'Cause these men don't get it
They don't hear the ignorance or feel the shame
As if my ethnicity alone defines me
As if I'm different from my Indian sisters
You're exotic and you have aryan features
A White man said to me in high school
While he laughed it off
Or the classic
You don't look Indian
Heard from various people
As if I should feel joy from a man finding me attractive
For my background
Not just White men
But men of color are guilty
Of making remarks like these as well
It is humiliating that women of color
Are still compared to White women
As an ideal standard of beauty
That I am only desirable because
I'm seen as exotic
That I can only be pretty
For an Indian girl
And not just pretty
On my own

— *The Stigma Behind: Pretty For An Indian Girl*

I have had to be
The men
I have a lack of
In my life

If they don't regularly check up on you
To make sure you're well
You're safe
If you're breathing
How can you call them
Your friends

To me
Writing isn't about
Fancy words
Or the meaning behind a piece
Being completely subtle
That you miss it
It's about explaining
What has happened to me
What is happening to me
Who I am
How I feel
In the simplest way
Possible
But not being simple
To take in

The abuse is what happened to you
But it does not define you
It is not who you are

— *Survivor*

I've suffered silently about things that
My mother is completely unaware of
Weeping at night secretly
I wonder how many things my mother
Has suffered quietly
That still remain a mystery
To me

How many times do I have to be told
Be happy
As if I can be just that
With the snap of a finger
'Cause there are days when the
Happiness
Doesn't come as easy

— *Happiness Isn't Always A Choice*

Growing up quiet
Has its challenges
I don't always speak
When I have something to say
I don't always get what I need
At times I've been shy to ask
I find it difficult to force conversation
Which makes me prefer silence
But those aren't the only challenges I've faced
For being quiet
Part of being quiet means I'm being misjudged
There are constant misconceptions being made
That I'm dense
Anti-social or cold
Perhaps arrogant or stuck up
Several conclusions are drawn about my essence
But none of them add up
To who I am

That's how humans are
We take so many things for granted
Mostly, each other

Hands
How much they tell
How much they hold
How much they let go

When they tell you that being Fijian
Or being Afghan
Being Pakistani
Being Persian
Anything that looks like what you *should be*
Are the same anyway
Is not just ignorance
When they don't let you finish saying
That they're wrong
Should not be tolerated
Because you wouldn't confuse
Germany for Ireland
France for Denmark
Britain for Norway
So why the hell
Is it okay
For them to assume
You come from the same place
As the people who may
Look like you
Yet know nothing about you

— *Same Difference*

Writing is a process that
Takes you to hell
Before it helps you
Heal

How is it possible to live in two extremes
To be a deep feeler
Yet remain detached
Simultaneously

What if eyes could speak
Oh, *but they do*

I melt with every touch
Every bite, every kiss
Every part of you
That makes me soft again

The way you say
My name
Echoes
In my mind
I spend days
Lost in a place
That makes me feel as safe as
The comfort of your voice

Every single person who comes into your life
Has two options
To stay or to leave
Isn't that scary to think about
That each person who has left your life
Had the choice to stay
Each person who has stayed
Still has the option to leave

Old souls recognize each other

From here
To wherever the last universe is
And the universe is always expanding so....
There is no end

— *When He Asked How Much I Love Him*

It was easy with you
We always started from
Wherever we left off
Skipping the small talk
For never ending conversations
Finishing each other's jokes
And sentences
Communicating with our eyes
During silent pauses
You don't get that type of connection often
But when you do
There are two fates to this equation
You either end up together
Like a chemical formula
Or
The chemistry stays
But the people
Don't

The way the moon
Makes love to the ocean
Leaves me in awe
They never touch each other
Yet I feel
The deep longing
Intimacy
Soul level connection
In each tide
That rushes up
To get close to her

— *Love & Light*

Spending long periods of
Time alone
Is both toxic
And liberating

— *Antisocial*

I force myself
To write
On days that I feel
Nothing

— *Therapy*

I find myself cutting corners
In my sentences
Rushing to finish
What I need to say
Before I am interrupted
It is such a force of habit
Sometimes I forget that there are
Those few
Active listeners
Who don't require me
To cut myself off

— *Predisposition To Silence*

When I withdraw
Or become angry at someone
It isn't because I don't care
In fact
The contrary may be taking place instead
I am just exhausted
From being the only one to care
So when I am waiting for someone
To initiate an apology
After I did my part
After I put in effort
I am not doing it 'cause of pride
Or revenge
Or immaturity
I care
I care so much
However
I want to see what extent they're willing to go
To show they care about me
Notice I didn't say
Care about me, *too*
'Cause frankly, I don't know
I really don't
This is how
Silent endings
Happen

Throughout the years
I've learned a thing or two
About putting people
In their place

— *Reevaluation*

There are infinite realities
Infinite dimensions
Where you and I exist
It hurts to know there are other universes
Besides this one
Where we still couldn't last

Time and time again
I have come to terms that
Soul connections don't mean
People won't become strangers
Soul connections don't always mean
Soul mate
Sometimes they're there to teach us
To go with our gut instinct
To not fall into something tempting
That if you've been patient for this long
You can do a little more waiting

We run back to the familiar
Because it made us
Feel something

— *The High*

Ritu Kaur

You have a way with words
Is both a compliment
And a curse
There's beauty in the struggle
That's what helped me
Write this verse

Men's opinions of you
Are as significant as
The specks of dust
We are made from

Most people would rather
Kiss up
To those who are already up there
'Cause of status or beauty or riches
The same people who reek of desperation
For attention
Neglecting to support their actual friends
The same ones who beg for
Endorsements from friends and strangers
Are giving credit to those who
Are already successful
And no support
To those
They know
I steer clear
From both
I'll make it up there
On my own

Sometimes *no* doesn't suffice with your soul
So you break the rules....

The life of an underdog
Is simple to understand
No one wants to support you
Until you're supported by
Thousands
Of strangers

The law of attraction
Is very real
For those who
Choose to believe in it
And especially for those
Who don't

— *Manifest Your Destiny*

Where there is love
There is everything
Even when you have nothing

— *Reminder From My Grandfather*

I've had dreams
Of poems
That I have not yet written
Knowing my subconscious
Is trying to show me something
Embedded deep inside of me
Communication from a dimension
That seems out of reach
When I wake up
I write to make my dreams
A reality

— *Messages In My Sleep*

Assumptions create
The most negative thoughts
The most misunderstandings
They cause us to jump to conclusions
'Cause as humans
We are so needy for
Endings
For reasoning
For clarity
That we blur out the clarity
And fill in the spots
With our toxic thoughts
To make sense out of whatever is
Happening to us
Not knowing we're creating harm
Within us and outside of us
'Cause we're so desperate for an end
So that reality makes sense
But all we're really doing is
Destroying
Human connections

Put yourself in my shoes
And not just for a second
Actually stop and think about what it feels like
To be *me* in this situation for at least five minutes
Don't just put on my shoes
Put on my clothes
My heart
My soul
Then tell me the same things you've been saying
'Cause I've thought about everything
From your view too much

— *Now I'm Tired*

Don't let people get you out of character
Because of their rudeness towards you
'Cause no one is worth the anger
Resentment
Or hate
We all have bad days
Sometimes the anger gets displaced
We should try to respect each other
During our short time on Earth
Since we all come with
Different
Expiration dates

Having chemistry
With the wrong person
Will bring out unrestricted parts of yourself
That you're afraid to bring out on your own
Do not mistake this for love

Our thoughts are radiating frequencies
That go out into the youniverse as
Little clouds of energy
It's important that your thoughts
Are as beautiful as your physicality
'Cause our thoughts shape us
Our lives and
Our reality

Those who make you question
Yourself
After they've left
As if there is something wrong
With you
Causing you to point out every flaw
You have
Just to get an answer as to why
People leave
Are completely empty themselves
They need you to join them
In their misery

— *You Are Full*

I'm not running away
From you
I am running
Past you
There is a
Difference

Love isn't enough
To keep two people together
There are sacrifices involved
Compromises to be made
A deeper understanding
A need
A desire
To keep the other person happy
Which sometimes makes us
Forget about
Our own happiness
Love is a foundation
It is the answer
But it doesn't always keep two people
Together

Unlearning is just as
Important as
Learning

They want you to
Do well
But they fail to support
Your well-doing

If the friendship
Relationship
Connection
Was important enough
They wouldn't solely rely
On you
To initiate
A heart to heart

— *Two Way Street*

I think I am too much of a woman
For most people
This makes me feel empowered

My mother did what she could
To teach my brothers
About respecting women
Anshi and I did what we could
To do the same
Now the courses of action
They take for
Or against women
Solely rely on them
For they are men raised with standards
And in no way
Should we have to
Take the blame

— *Ignorance Is A Choice*

To be a provider for children
Who aren't yours
Is heroic

— *To My Stepfather*

Someday
The Earth won't be here
And you're letting something
As small as
Someone else's opinion of you
Or societal standards
Anything that doesn't add value
To your life
Get in the way of living
80 years on Earth is a short time
Yet 80 years in this world is a long time
To not do what you want
If you're even guaranteed
80 years
To begin with

I feel a collection of waves forming inside of me every time I am hurt. Until I can no longer contain that hurt. My body trembles. My eyes create a tsunami. And only then do I feel a sense of peace. Maybe that's why tsunamis occur on earth. When our planet is so hurt. She does nothing. She can't do anything. Except cry.

We leave just as we came
Bringing nothing with us
Taking nothing with us
Nothing in this life or universe is permanent
Except for you and I

Isn't it crazy when you witness
Girls complimenting each other
Saying good things to everyone
Except you
Ganging up making it feel like
A competition
Making you feel like
You aren't good enough
Smart enough
Pretty enough
Not that you're fishing for
Compliments or validation
You are more than enough
But all along there was silence
Towards you
Out of jealousy

— *False Friendships*

Why do I feel more hurt
When they tell me
What I feel is normal
That whatever is happening to me
Happens to others
As if that is some sort of justification
For what I feel
For what I'm going through
Yes, it may be true
That others deal with what I do
That others have dealt with worse
Still that doesn't mean
I don't feel the pain of my experience
That my pain isn't present
'Cause it is

Getting out of bed
Was a fight between
The part of me that cared
With the part of me that didn't
There were wins
There were losses
Not knowing how long I slept
Was another daily struggle
That merged with not sleeping enough
Overeating
Or not eating for days
Losing track of time
After watching countless movies
Taking long walks with no destination
Having no friends was the biggest downfall
Being in a bad place
Mentally
Emotionally
Physically
Being lost in clouded thoughts
Not knowing my purpose
Not caring about anything or anyone
Wondering when I'd die
Why I was alive
Hating everyone
Including myself
The never ending battle
Between my head
And my heart

— *Depression*

My twelfth grade English teacher told me
It's normal to think about death once in a while
And thinking about it excessively is unhealthy
But how do you take that in as a 17-year-old
When did it start becoming unhealthy to think of death
As the last thing on your mind
Before falling asleep
When did death become the first thing you think of
In the morning
'Cause you're disappointed for waking up again

The pressure started
When Mummy Ji came here
With her parents
It continued with her first born
Since I am supposed to be
Worth the leave
Worth the sacrifices
Worth the blood, sweat, tears
I am supposed to be
The hero
That I *still*
Am not

— *First Generation Graduate*

I am so often misunderstood
I have grown
Tired
Of explaining
And when people don't ask for
An explanation
I let them choose
The ending

— *I Don't Owe Anyone An Explanation For Anything*

If there's one thing my father taught me
It's that I didn't want to grow up to be a coward

As humans we're temporary
But so is the Earth
And our surrounding planets
Our solar system
The galaxy
Infinite universes
Yes, we are expanding
Just like the universe
Everything has to change
In order to
Grow

To see Mummy Ji read my writing and shed tears. Has never made me feel more connected or humble. Her pain is my pain. My pain is hers. To know that another human being understands. What it's like. Not just Mummy Ji. Not just Mannu, Dev or Anshi. But everyone who takes the time to read my work. Those who say it means something. That my words touch them. To see that pain in physical form. The tears. To see the feelings emerge in goosebumps. Leaves me speechless. I have no words. And normally I'd be able to explain how I'm feeling. But I am dumbstruck. Overwhelmed. Making this experience a whole different language. So I thank you for this beauty I can't explain. This language I can't translate.

— *The Realest Things Aren't Seen, Only Felt*

Whoever said that love hurts
Is only suffering from an absence
Of love
Love heals
Love conquers
Love transcends
It is the only thing
Feeling
Vibration
That can travel through
Space
Time
Gravity
The only thing
Feeling
Energy
We desire most
Love does not hurt
But the absence of love
Now, that
Is a
Tragedy

I've stopped taking the blame
For people who have walked out of my life
For those who will walk out of my life
To those who have lost me
To those who will lose me
I'd like to apologize for any misunderstandings
'Cause if I was able to see something beautiful in you
I only wish you could have witnessed the same in me
I'd like to apologize for your clouded vision
The way I am able to forgive, understand and listen
Is a precious gift many take for granted
'Cause people forget a heart that understands
Is also a heart that becomes exhausted
I am drained from being the one to initiate contact
Weary of being the one who loves unconditionally
So I won't see you differently
I thought that because of these things
Because of my traits
People could see my intentions
That people would see the real me
But I am done trying to please everyone
'Cause I know my worth
'Cause I deserve the same love I give in return
'Cause I am still able to love deeply
No matter how much I hurt
So for those of you who think I am
Crazy, weird, or mad
I know who I am
I'm just waiting for someone to truly understand

— *I'm A Superwoman*

I didn't write this book
To complain about life
Or to talk about my past
Or to put the blame on others
We all feel pain
We all have a story
I wrote this book
To let you know
You are not alone
In yours

There's a societal clock.
That we are expected to follow.
To graduate college. In our early twenties.
To get a decent job. By mid-twenties.
Marriage in late twenties. Kids before thirty.
But if you can ignore the fact.
That you're not a part of that race.
That we all have different paths.
If you can subside the feeling. Of being lost. Or behind.
That in the midst of all the chaos.
You can continue to stay. On your journey. At peace.
Then you have learned. What the soul already knows.
You're timeless.

I don't want to work
9-5
Just to pay bills and
Stay alive

Sobering up from
The shrooms
In Hawai'i
Made real life
Feel like a nightmare
The profound laughter
I couldn't control
Came from layers deep inside of me
The tickling sensation in my legs
That wouldn't allow me to sleep
Dancing to the drums played by
The tribal folks on the beach
I understood why people
Develop dependency

— *Magic Mushies*

I had been aching for years
From loneliness
It's what helped me
Look within
To find a
Goddess

My focus has shifted from
How others perceive me
To how I perceive myself

— *Priorities*

What I cannot fully take in
What I cannot fully understand is
Why as humans
We label things or people
That have left our lives
As losses
As if things are permanent
As if people are our property
As if people don't have the power
To lead their own lives without us
That when family ties end
Or friendships fail
We claim that we lost a person
Or they lost us
As if there was some sort of mutual ownership
I am guilty of wording endings this way myself
So instead
From now on I will say things like
Our paths no longer align
Or their part in my journey is over
Or simply that we are now strangers
Since everything is temporary
No one belongs to me
I belong to
No one
And because of this
I will not face any type of loss again
'Cause I have taken away the power for it to happen

He wanted to leave
I didn't let him
He wanted to leave
I couldn't let him
He wanted to leave
I begged him
He wanted to leave
I left him

I'm attracted to mystery
Which leaves me telling people
Bits and pieces about myself
Letting them fill in a few blanks
About who they think I am
I do this for the sole purpose of
Allowing people to feel like
They have me figured out
It's crazy how much people think
They know me
'Cause I've given them the power
To feel this way
While they unknowingly remain on the
Surface

— *Selective Sharing*

Have you ever noticed that
The people who have gone through
The most struggle
Don't talk about it
Instead they
Tend to release it
Through a form of
Art
To depict
Highlight
Make sense of it all
In beauty
Instead of chaos

— *To My Writers, Artists, Creators*

Spirituality has taught me
That the religion
Humans should follow
Is love
It has taught me to speak
The language of love
Through spirituality
I have learned
To breathe love
To spread love
To be love
I hear it from the voices
Up above
If love is the inevitable answer
Why have we not
Started there
Yet

The hearts of my people
Are compared to the hearts of lions
Bold
Brave
Resilient

— *Sikh*

I see my mother's body aching from
Years of being on her feet
Her heart is still as big as the day she had me
I think about the stories she has told me
About herself from when
She was back home in the motherland
She was six years old when she used to eat her lunch
Every morning on the bus on her way to school
Then during lunch she'd stare at other kids
Eating their lunches since her bag was already empty
In the summers she and her brother
Would take mangos from the neighbor's trees
Typical sibling habits that would get them into trouble
A few months before the attacks in 1984
She left the motherland with her family
For an opportunity known as the *American dream*
She stopped doing her homework for months
Her logic being that she was leaving for the U.S. any day
Her teacher wasn't pleased with her reasoning
She was eleven
A year after being in the states she was diagnosed
With cancer
She was told she would never have children
When she was sixteen she ran away from home
To avoid marriage
She was found two weeks later and
Forced to marry a cheater
At nineteen she went to the hospital
For severe abdominal pain
She found out she was six months pregnant
She had her first child in 1992
Ritu
The name that made sense to her for her first daughter
Almost 25 years later
I'm sitting here wishing that I met my mother sooner

Give me light
And I will grow hundreds
Possibly a thousand times more
Give me darkness
I will grow
Infinitely

I don't have backup plans
I think on my feet
This is how I've come across
Serendipity

As a woman
I have an innate knowledge
A profound understanding of love
All types of love
As a daughter
As a sister
As a future wife
As a future mother
As a nurturer
It's an understanding that gives me an advantage
To be able to connect with others
On a deeper level without much effort
It's also an understanding that hurts me
For the women
Who don't tap into this potential

When you put yourself down
When you don't see the beauty
Only you hold
The miraculous space
You take
You've forgotten
That you are here
Existing
Through a force
That believes in you
How can you not
Believe in it

What is it about the night sky.
That gives humans the courage to.
Share dark parts. Of themselves.
What is it about the sunny sky.
To keep these things hidden.
From each other.
In broad daylight
We hide ourselves.
At nighttime we whisper.
Our secrets.

— 3am

That eye contact connection
You have with someone
That only you two know about
The tension
The mystery
If there will ever be anything more
Than just
Eye contact
Every time you pass by
Each other

These vivid dreams
I keep having about you
Almost makes me believe
You want to see us
Together, too

Finding my way
To you
Through the midst
Of all the chaos
Through all of the
Distance
Between us
Every time I am lost
Again and
Again
That's gravity

Light.
That is
What you
Taste like

Waves, like words
Is the language of the ocean
With each wave that crashed onto shore
Some were light and refreshing
Washing away the dirt
Some waves were like mini tsunamis
Misunderstood
Crashing hard
Consuming me
Like the ocean was furious
At what we were doing to 75% of the earth
At what we were doing to the ocean
At what we were doing to our home

— *The Ocean is Alive*

We're amnesiacs
When we look into infinity
We have forgotten
That we are the clusters of light
That brighten the endless sky
The galaxies that have been birthed
To create new worlds
We have forgotten
That we are the moon
And the sun
The lights that seem small
From far away
But light your heart on fire
If you come too close
We are a reflection of the sky
Mere passers-by in this realm
We are cloudy skies
And rainy nights
We are the stars
That don't dim
We are the stars
We wish we could travel to
We are the stars
That we look up to
On nights when we realize
Our problems are small
We are the stars

The waves and I
Have something in common
There is consistency
In our flow

I recognized myself
After letting go
After healing
Seeing my familiar self
With more compassion
Love
Understanding
Holding myself
It was okay now
I was finally home

The most exhilarating part about writing
The most connecting thing
About ten different people
Reading what I wrote
Is that my poem
Now has
Ten different meanings

I need someone
Who understands me
Someone who has been through
Shit
Someone who knows
What struggle is
Someone who has gotten the
Short end of the stick
Someone who didn't quit
Someone who doesn't make fun of
Another person
For having a fake branded bag
I need someone who cares about
The things that matter
The things that aren't things
I need someone who knows what I need
Without me having to explain
Someone who feels that my pain
Is also their struggle
I need someone to need me
Just as much as I need them
Without the attachment
Someone who knows what I've been through
And doesn't feel sympathy
But respect

— *Someone Like Me*

I don't want any gifts
Unless your definition of a gift is
Giving me your time in exchange for me
Taking a flight with me
In or out of country
Over mountains or over the deep blue sea
If your understanding of a gift
Are kisses to wake me up from my sleep
And long hugs when I need to cry
Without either of us
Having to say anything
If your meaning of a gift is
Putting thought into me
Listening to my passions and my fears
And still seeing me for me
If what you think of as a gift is
Surprising me with a candle lit picnic in your backyard
Or going to the beach for a long walk
If it's you writing me a letter
Or us coming home to each other
Being present for one another
Because your presence is already a gift
If any of these *things* on my list
Are what a gift means to you
Then I will gladly accept
'Cause the things that aren't things
Make me the happiest
The intangible things
That we'll get to experience

— A Letter To My Future Lover

He never knew
I wrote a poem
About him
Nonetheless,
That he was a poem
Himself

I want to be with someone
Who knows he has me
But doesn't stop trying
In order to keep me

I can't wait to be
In your arms
I can already feel
Your warmth

— *When I Meet My Soul Mate*

Some of life's luckiest moments
Happen
When you are alone
They leave you
So grateful
All you can do
Is cry

— *Happy Tears*

I used to judge people
Through the words they spoke
Or from the actions they took
But I now step in peoples' shoes
To see life from their view
Learning that we all act according to
The situations that we've been through
Making it difficult for me
To hate anyone
Because I understand human behavior
Too much

— *Higher Thinking*

Appreciation.
The secret ingredient.
The key foundation.
The cliché and yet unused method.
For a full life.

Your words are like an arrow was shot at the heart

— When Mummy Ji Reads My Writing

I pray in this lifetime
That I receive a
Father's love
In my next

What people fail to understand
About loving yourself is
How long it took you
To get there

— *Work In Progress*

I base my success on
My level of happiness

For what is truth, but a different perspective? Is there one truth to anything? Do we translate languages based on our general understanding? Do we view something based on our experiences? Do we take into account another person's past, present, socioeconomic status, their level of education, their level of ignorance? If I look at the sunset from a 90 degree angle, are you seeing what I'm seeing, from your 60 degree angled view? Is there a truth to anything— is there such a thing as a lie— or is there merely just, perception?

— *More Questions*

Healing isn't always a pretty process
People think it's about smiling and
Pretending you're okay
Sometimes that's a must
Because you can't dwell in a place
That doesn't exist
You must move on
And you will
At your own pace, every single day
But healing isn't pretty
It destroys everything you once
Believed in
Loved
Knew
Yet it allows things to fall
Beautifully into place
It brings you closer to
Your truest
Self

— *Full Potential*

The first wave started when I thought
Being fondled with was love
The second wave started
When I heard Mummy fighting with the stranger
Who was supposed to be dad
The third wave came when Mummy was blamed
For the fondling
Stripping us away from her and putting us in a home
With more danger
The fourth wave occurred when Mummy separated
From the stranger
And got with another man who couldn't control his anger
The blackmail and stalking
I was followed to school
Mom was followed home
Five years later, there was a restraining order
The sixth wave came when I met him
Thinking I'd never find a love more pure
Than the one I was in
The seventh wave arrived silently
Making me look deeper within
Just when I thought I was done healing
Someone broke me again
The eighth wave arrived silently
I've been patiently waiting
Praying and writing
Gradually healing
The next wave will be greater
'Cause I don't know what to expect
From the waves of the ocean
Which bring up the past
While also washing away anything in their way
But these waves that have happened
Have made me who I am
I'm not scared of the ocean
I always dive in
'Cause these waves and I have a rough past
These waves of the ocean
Taught me how to swim

It is a relief
And an accomplishment
To be able to
Put the
Hurt
Into words

Love.
That's what I'm
Made up
Of

I've washed yesterday, yesteryear, and the last two decades away. Freshening up. Letting tears flow just as much as I laugh. Dancing in the rain. Soaking in the sun. Seeing a new part of the world every summer. Seeing a new world in myself every day. Allowing old friendships to fail 'cause they were never real in the first place. Making friends out of strangers online 'cause people far away tend to be more supportive. Used to being a loner. Living in solitude. Living within the community. Living. Not just existing. Genuinely living.

— *The Earth Has Orbited Once Again*

If my writing makes you
Feel something
It is not I,
Who has done justice

— *Thank you*

In the end
We are not who others perceive us to be
We are those who live by what we do
And stand by what we say
'Cause if those things are in consistency
Who can tell us otherwise?
Live by your own rules
That is
If you choose to have any
And most importantly
Love those who love you
There's enough hate that goes around
But love
Love is precious
It is the only logical answer
You are love
Don't be afraid to spread a little bit of yourself to others
We could use more love
More of you
You came into this world for a reason
But it's not for a reason
That you need to live for
You figure that out when you ride along this wave
Your wave
In this sea of life
Keep sailing and swimming
Keep diving and kicking
The big waves may delay your journey
But it's the collection of little waves that
You'll remember most

— *Until We Meet Again*

About the author & the book:

Ritu Kaur, also known as Tajinder Kaur Sekhon, is a Punjabi writer from the bay area, California. She published her first book, *Waves*, as a self-tribute for turning 25.

Waves is a collection of poetry, which includes themes of abuse, relationships, sexism, misogyny, racism and getting through life's waves no matter how tough the sea of life can be.

To stay connected with Ritu's writing and latest updates, please visit www.instagram.com/tjsyouniverse